The
AMERICAN
SCHOOLHOUSE READER

*A Colorized Children's Reading Collection
from Post-Victorian America
1890 - 1925*

BOOK III

Editing and Colorized Illustrations
by Beverly Allie

ISBN: 0-9747615-0-8 (3 Volume Set)

Printed in Hong Kong
First Printing 2004

Published by 45th Parallel Concepts
www.americanschoolhousereader.com

PREFACE

This book is one of three volumes in the first Colorized Vintage Reader Collection. This unique set contains selections from children's readers used in American schools during the late 19th and early 20th centuries. In this collection you will find many sweet stories and reading exercises adorned with old fashioned values, and a quality of culture that has been lost.

The illustrations, as well, are reflections of a day when craftsmanship was the standard. The authentic black and white woodcuts and line drawings that graced the pages of these readers have been beautifully painted in color. A number of illustrations which were originally printed in color have also been repainted in new colors.

Young children will love them as charming picture books and will enjoy having the stories read aloud to them. Parents and teachers will welcome the series as delightful reading material for children of different ages and levels of reading skill.

In this collection, children will read about nature, pets, farms and families, and will learn something of what it was like to live during the post-Victorian era. Poems, skits and several stories about historic figures have also been included. Young readers will relive a time when life was different, when life was simpler, and when children had far fewer negative influences than they have today.

The wonderful stories and wholesome principles in this collection, combined with the rare charm and quality found in the color illustrations, will make these books a welcome addition to any home or school library.

PART I

*D*erived from

THE LEARN TO STUDY READERS, BOOK ONE
by Ernest Horn and Grace Shields
Ginn and Company, 1924

PART II

*D*erived from

STORIES OLD AND NEW
by Abigail O. Sheriff
Ginn and Company, 1922

Part III

*D*erived from

STORY-LAND DRAMATIC READER
by Catherine T. Bryce
Charles Scribner's Sons, 1916

Part IV

*D*erived from

TALES OUT OF SCHOOL
by Myra King
Educational Publishing Company, 1911

PART I

CONTENTS

WATER

What is it that firemen must have to put out a fire? The firemen need water to put out fires. When there is a fire, the fire engine comes quickly. The firemen fasten their hose to the hydrant. They throw water on the burning house. Soon the fire is put out.

In what other ways does water help us? Have you ever been very thirsty? How long do you think you could live without water to drink? No one could live long without it. Even the milk we drink has water in it.

Everyone should drink plenty of water. Most people do not drink enough water. Animals, too, must have water.

In some countries where water is very scarce, there are men that carry water around to sell to people. The man in the picture is carrying water in a sack. The sack is made of leather. He sells water to anyone who is thirsty.

The water that comes down as rain makes plants grow. The picture at the top of this page shows a country where there is plenty of rain. When there is not enough rain, plants do not grow well. Look at the picture at the bottom of this page. This country does not have enough rain to make plants grow well.

Have you ever been on a boat? Boats travel on the water. Large ships sail only on the ocean, on large lakes, and on large rivers. Smaller boats sail on smaller rivers and lakes. They also sail on the ocean and on large lakes and rivers.

The water makes the wheel of the mill go around. It pushes against the paddle of the wheel. This makes the wheel turn. The wheel turns other wheels in the mill.

This picture shows a water wheel of an old mill. Farmers brought corn to this mill to be ground into meal. Some wheels turn saws which cut logs into lumber.

If we had no water, we could have no ice. Ice helps us to keep our food fresh. Some ice is made in ice factories. Much ice is taken from lakes and rivers in the winter.

Men saw the ice into blocks. They put it into ice houses. They cover it with sawdust so that it will not melt. In summer, when it is hot, the ice man brings it to our homes.

Water helps us to keep clean and healthy. We need it to bathe in. We need it to wash our clothes. We use it in washing our dishes and in cleaning our floors and windows. Cities use it in washing the streets and sidewalks.

How should you like to be here? Most boys and girls like to wade in the water when it is warm and play in the sand. Water makes sand out of rocks by rubbing them together. The water then brings the sand to the shore.

WIND

What are these children doing? Have you ever had a kite? Have you tried to fly it on a windy day? It is great fun. The wind makes the kite go.

Wind is air that is moving. When the air moves slowly, there is not much wind. When it moves swiftly, we say that the wind blows hard.

We cannot see the wind, but we can see what the wind does. We can see trees bend. We can see the leaves and papers scatter. When we are outdoors, we can feel it push against us. Can you think of other things which the wind does?

Have you seen the wind turn a windmill? In Holland, most windmills pump water for the farmer. They help him a great deal. In this country, the windmills help the farmer churn his cream and grind his grain. Holland is a country across the ocean.

Wind makes some kinds of ships go. These ships have sails. The wind blows against the sails. It pushes the ships through the water.

Not all ships have sails. Most large ships now have engines in them. Many small boats have gas engines. These engines burn gasoline. Some boats have sails and an engine, too.

In the autumn the wind blows the leaves from the trees and sends them whirling to the ground. Did you ever try to catch leaves as they blow from the trees? It is a good sport.

The wind blows the leaves into piles against fences and buildings. It is fun to jump into piles of leaves. Most children like to play in the autumn leaves.

The wind brings the rain and snow. If we had no wind, we should have no rain or snow. The wind blows the clouds to us.

The wind also makes it cool. In summer, the nights are pleasant when the wind blows. In the winter, the north wind makes it very cold.

The wind is not always our friend. In winter it makes deep snowdrifts in the streets and in the roads. Have you ever helped to make a path through the snow? This picture shows how sidewalks are sometimes cleared of snow.

In some places, the wind makes snowdrifts on the railroad track. Sometimes the drifts are so deep that the trains cannot run. The trains must wait until the drifts are cleared away.

The wind makes drifts of sand. This is a picture of a desert. A desert is so dry that few things can grow there. When the wind blows hard in a desert, the air is filled with sand. It blows the sand into great drifts. You can see drifts of sand in this picture.

The wind makes storms at sea. It blows against the water. It makes great waves in the water. You can see them in the picture. Sometimes the great waves sink a ship. Sometimes a ship is blown against hard rocks. It is hard for a ship to sail in a storm.

Sometimes the wind blows very hard on land. It blows the limbs of trees over. It blows down the telephone wires. It blows the farmer's haystacks over. It plays pranks on us, too. It turns our umbrellas wrong side out. It blows our hats off. It scatters our papers all about.

The wind scatters seeds everywhere. Many of these seeds are weed seeds. Many seeds have little wings. The maple seed has broad, flat wings. The dandelion seed has fluffy wings. The wind blows these seeds all around. What seeds that have wings have you seen?

ABRAHAM LINCOLN

All children loved Abraham Lincoln. Do you know why? It was because he was always kind. He was kind to children and to grown-up people. He was kind to animals, too. He could not bear to see an animal suffer.

One day Lincoln was riding along a country road. He was with some other men. The road was very muddy. All at once they saw a pig stuck in a mud hole. It was trying hard to get out, and it was squealing as loud as it could. The men laughed at the pig. They thought it looked funny. Do you think that Lincoln laughed? No, he felt sorry for the pig.

He rode on with the men for a little while. He could not forget the poor pig that was trying so hard to get out of the mud.

At last he turned around and rode quickly back to help the pig. He took some rails from a fence. With their help he lifted the pig out of the mud. It was not hurt at all. The pig ran off, flapping its ears and grunting happily.

But you should have seen Lincoln's clothes! They were covered with mud. When the men saw Lincoln, they began to laugh. They knew that he did not often have a new suit of clothes. They told him he was foolish to do so much for a pig.

Lincoln said to them, "That farmer's children might have to go barefoot next winter if he lost his pig." Do you know what he meant?

ARBOR DAY

Arbor Day means "tree day." It is a special day for planting trees. Trees are useful as well as beautiful. They shade us from the summer's sun. Birds build nests in trees.

The color and shape of the trees help to make our country beautiful. In the spring they are a pretty green, and in the fall they have many beautiful colors.

The hard maple is one of the best shade trees. It has blossoms which the bees like. The sap of this tree is very sweet. Early in the spring people tap this tree to get maple sap. This sap may be boiled down until it becomes maple sugar.

Some trees are always green. They are called evergreens. Our Christmas trees are evergreen trees. The names of some of the evergreens are spruce, fir and pine.

What do trees give us for our homes? Trees give us lumber for our houses. They give us lumber for the furniture, too.

This picture shows men cutting down trees. The trees will be made into lumber.

Trees give us many things which we use every day. The paper in this book is made from wood. Wood is used in making your pencils, chair and desk. Can you think of other things which are made of wood?

Trees are sometimes used for fuel. Do you burn wood to heat your home? How many uses for wood can you see in this picture?

What do trees give us to eat? Trees give us many kinds of seeds which can be used for food. Walnuts, hickory nuts, chestnuts, pecans and almonds grow on trees. The acorns from oak trees are eaten by hogs and squirrels. The squirrels do not eat all the nuts. Children like to eat nuts, too.

Trees give us fruit, too. Apples, peaches, cherries and pears grow on trees. Fruit trees grow in all parts of our country. Oranges, lemons, olives and figs also grow on trees. They grow only where it is warm. What fruit have you seen growing on trees?

This is a picture of a forest fire. Thousands of trees are burned in forest fires each year. Many such fires are caused by careless people who throw lighted matches on the ground. Some fires are caused by people who do not put out their camp fires. Sometimes fires are started by sparks from a train. A fire may be started even by lightning.

This is a picture of land where the trees have been cut down. Many, many trees are cut down each year. Every year we should plant new trees to take the place of those that have been cut down or burned.

In 1872, a man named Julius Sterling Morton asked the people in his state of Nebraska to have a special day for planting trees. More than a million trees were planted on that day. Now all the states have a day for planting trees. This day is called Arbor Day.

WOOL

My winter coat and the winter coats of sheep do not look very much alike, but Mother says the sheep's winter coat can be made into a warm winter coat for me.

This curly winter coat of the sheep is called wool. When the spring days come, the sheep are too hot with such a warm coat. I find my winter coat too warm also when spring days come. I brush it and lay it away in the cedar chest.

The sheep cannot lay off their coats so easily. They must have help. How is the wool taken off the sheep? Men have to cut off the wool. This is called shearing the sheep. Shearing is done in two ways.

The old way to cut off the wool is with hand shears. These shears look like a large pair of scissors. The wool cannot be cut off very evenly with a pair of shears. It takes a long time to shear sheep this way.

Most men now use a machine to shear the sheep. This machine cuts off the wool evenly and quickly. Many sheep can be sheared by a machine while one is being sheared in the old way. If you had a large flock of sheep, how would you shear them?

Is the wool now ready for Mother to make it into a coat? No, many things must first be done to it. It must be washed and cleaned. It must be dyed. It must be made into yarn. The yarn must be made into cloth. Then it will be ready to be made into a coat.

TELEPHONE MANNERS

I answer the telephone at our house. This helps Mother and Father very much. When the bell rings, I run quickly to the telephone. If someone wishes to speak to Mother, I say, "I will call her." Sometimes Mother is not at home. Then I say, "Mother is not at home just now. May I take your message?"

When someone gives me a message, I try to remember just what is told to me. I give the message to Mother as soon as she comes home.

If someone wishes to leave a number, I write it neatly on a piece of paper and put the paper where Mother or Father will be sure to see it.

Dear Mother, please call up Mrs. Lane as soon as you come home, River 604J.
Martha

SIGNS

Do you know what a sign is?   What are signs for? Tell about some signs that you have seen. On the previous page you will see some signs. Try to find where each of these signs belongs.

FREE AIR

DANGER!

GAS

FOR SALE

FOR RENT

ROAD CLOSED

SCHOOL - GO SLOW

HOUSE TO LET

STOP! LOOK! LISTEN!

DO NOT PARK HERE

ROOM FOR RENT

ROOM AND BOARD

LOOK OUT FOR THE CARS

PART II

CONTENTS

BETSY ROSS
AND THE FLAG

Betsy Ross lived in the city of Philadelphia from 1752 to 1836.

One day General Washington came to see if she would make a flag for the United States. He said that it was time the country had a flag of its own. He also told her that he had heard of her beautiful sewing.

She was pleased to be asked to make a flag for General Washington and said that she would do her best.

General Washington then said that the colors of the flag were to be red, white and blue. There were to be thirteen stripes, seven red and six white. In a corner of the flag there was to be a blue field with thirteen white stars on it. He had cut some paper stars to show her what he wanted. The stars had six points.

When Betsy Ross saw the stars that Washington had cut out, she said that they would look better if they had five points. She cut a five-pointed star for General Washington.

It was so pretty that he told her to make them all that way. When the flag was finished, he liked it very much.

By and by more states were added to our country and more stripes and stars were added to the flag. The flag did not look so well as it did before, and someone thought that it would be better to add only a star for every new state, and not a stripe. So the thirteen stripes were left as at first.

On Arch Street in Philadelphia the home of Betsy Ross still stands. Many who go to that city visit the old house whcrc the first United States flag was made.

HOME AGAIN !

"Why can't Hero go with us?" asked Mary and Jack, almost in one breath. "We are going too far to take a dog," said their father. "We will buy another dog when we reach our new home."

"But," the children cried, "no other dog can be half so good as Hero. He has always been with us, and we love him."

Hero had lived with the Brown family ever since Mary and Jack were little babies. He had played with them and later had gone to school with them. Hero knew how to do exactly as he was told. When Mr. Brown did not want Hero to go with him, and the dog would start to follow, Mr. Brown would say, "Go home, Hero," and Hero would obey.

"Oh, please, father, let Hero go! We will take care of him and not let him trouble anyone on the train. He will be friends with everyone and we want him with us when we reach our new home."

The children wanted so much to keep their pet that Mr. Brown said he would think about it. "He will have to ride in the baggage car if he goes, and you can see him only once each day," said their father.

Mr. and Mrs. Brown, with their children, lived in a little Iowa town, but they were going to move to the Far West.

Next morning, Mr. Brown told his children that he had decided to take Hero with them, and a few days later they started for their new home.

Hero rode for two days and two nights in the baggage car. Mr. Brown and Jack and Mary went in to see him every day. The men on the train liked Hero because he was very friendly and seemed to enjoy riding on the cars.

When Jack and Mary came to see him, he barked joyfully; but when they went back into their car, he always tried to go with them. Then Mr. Brown would say, "Hero!" and Hero knew that he must stay where he was.

At last the journey came to an end. An automobile was waiting for the Brown family. In this they rode fifty miles to a ranch, where Mary and Jack's uncle lived. There they stayed for a few days. One morning their uncle took them all in his automobile many miles over the prairie to see the Western country.

Hero followed the car some distance before being noticed. Then Mr. Brown called, "Go home, Hero," expecting the dog to go back to the place from which he had set out. The children shouted, "Wait at home for us, Hero, good dog."

But Hero knew only one home, and to that home he started to go. He walked and trotted all that day and many other days.

Being just a little dog, he never will be able to tell all that he saw on his homeward trip. There may have been some kind people who threw him a bone, and there may have been some boys and girls who said a pleasant word to the little traveling dog.

Three months after the time that Hero had been taken on the train, he returned to the little town where the Browns had formerly lived.

Poor Hero was very thin and tired. He went to the house he had known as home, and barked and scratched at the door. A little girl opened the door and called, "Oh, Mother, see the dear little dog."

Hero was hungry and tired from his long journey, so these people fed him and let him sleep in their barn. In a few days Hero looked better. Then the neighbors said, "This dog looks like Hero Brown."

When Hero heard his name, he jumped and barked and almost talked. Someone wrote to Mr. Brown that Hero had come back to his old home. Very soon a letter came from Mr. Brown, telling how sad the children had been over losing their pet and how they had missed him.   Mr. Brown enclosed money to have Hero sent by express, and in less than a week, the dog was in the new home of the Brown children.

It would be hard to tell which were the happier, Jack and Mary with their dog friend and playfellow, or Hero himself.

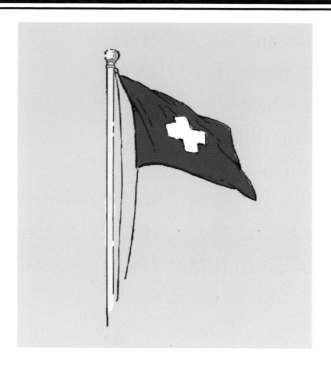

HENRI DUNANT
AND THE RED CROSS

Many years ago there was no Red Cross Society, and when soldiers were sick or hurt in war, there were very few people to take care of them and help them to get well.

A great battle was fought in Europe one summer at a place called Solferino. Henri Dunant, a kind man who lived in Switzerland, was visiting near Solferino. After the battle he went to the field where the wounded soldiers lay.

He was so sorry for them that he went to work himself, and some peasant women helped him. These women knew little about nursing, but were glad to help.

Mr. Dunant talked to the soldiers, bought them food and drink and medicine, and wrote letters for them to their homes. The soldiers loved him for his kindness and called him their good friend.

As soon as he could, Mr. Dunant wrote a book which told all about these soldiers whom he had helped, and said that everyone ought to be willing to do as much as they could for the brave men who were fighting for their country.

After the book had been written, Mr. Dunant went to many cities in Europe and told the people what should be done for those who serve in the army. He invited several men to meet him at his home to talk over plans for caring for sick and wounded or crippled soldiers.

These people decided to form themselves into a society which should provide such things as the soldiers in camps or in battle needed. They made Mr. Dunant their president.

They chose as their badge a white button with a red cross on it, and they named their society the Red Cross. They did this because their first meeting was held in Switzerland, and the flag of that country has a cross on it. The Swiss flag, however, has a white cross on a red background.

At first the Red Cross worked only on battlefields, but now it goes wherever large numbers of people are sick with no one to nurse them, or where earthquakes or fires or floods have caused great suffering. Red Cross workers make the sufferers comfortable and bring them food and clothing.

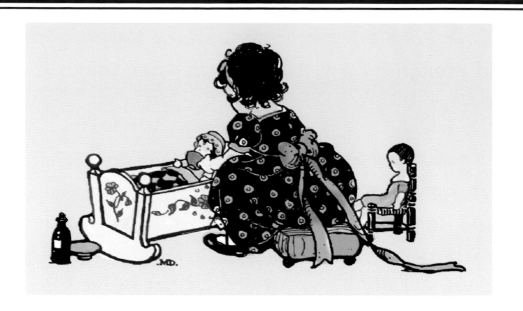

FLORENCE NIGHTINGALE

There was once a little girl whose name was Florence Nightingale. She was born in the beautiful city of Florence, Italy, and was named Florence for that city.

She loved to play at nursing and often pretended that her dolls were sick and that she must take care of them.

One day she heard that a poor shepherd's dog had broken its leg. She begged to be taken to see the dog.

"Florence, what can you do to save the life of a dog?" she was asked. "I don't know, but maybe I could do something," she answered.

At last her father went with her to see the dog. He found that the dog's leg was not broken and said that with care the little animal would get well.

"Let me help take care of him," Florence begged. Her father let her bathe the dog's leg, and she helped to put on a bandage. The dog licked her hand as if he wished to say, "Thank you, kind nurse; I feel much better."

Soon the dog was able to help his master tend the sheep. The shepherd was very grateful to

Florence. He said she had saved the life of his most helpful friend.

Florence's father had several bird houses which were always full in the summer. Sometimes the young birds would fall out of their nests and get hurt. Florence would run to them and care for them until they could get back to their nests again. They seemed to know that Florence was their friend, and never acted afraid of her. One summer she had a bird hospital where she tended more than twenty little birds.

Florence was so fond of flowers that her father gave her a garden of her own. Here she tended plants, digging about them and watering them carefully.

When a plant drooped or seemed about to die Florence would prop it up and call it her sick flower. Then she put fresh earth around it and, watered it. If the sun was too bright, she would shield the plant; or if she thought that it did not have enough sunshine, she would put it where it could get more. She said that her plants were like birds and children.

These sick plants often grew to be as strong as they were before. The family used to call Florence's garden the flower hospital, and she would say, "When I am grown up, I am going to have a hospital where all the sick can come to get well."

When Florence grew to be a woman, she studied to be a nurse. For a long time she cared for many sick people who lived near her home.

Then there was a great war and Florence went to the battlefield and took care of the soldiers who were sick and wounded. Many of these men were so grateful to their nurse that they gave large sums of money to build a hospital for her, where she could tend those who were not well and who had no money to pay for doctors, nurses and medicine. This hospital was named the Florence Nightingale Hospital. At last, Florence had just what she had always said she would have.

Florence was happy when she heard about the Red Cross. She gave much money for it and did everything she could to help it.

CLARA BARTON

Everyone who knows about the American Red Cross has heard of Clara Barton. She was its first president.

Her best-loved playfellow when she was a little girl was her younger brother, David.

They were both fond of animals and had cats, dogs, chickens and birds for pets. They took very good care of their animals and trained some of them to do clever tricks.

Mr. Barton, their father, owned many fine horses, and David and Clara knew how to ride. Often they were seen riding across the country.

One day David fell from his horse and was so badly hurt that for two years he was not able to walk. That was a long time for anyone to be sick.

"During those years," he said, "Clara was my best nurse, for she seemed to know just what to do. She stayed with me most of the time and helped to care for me and amuse me."

She played games with him when he was able to play, and read to him when he wished her to. She gave him his medicine, carried him his food, and in all ways showed herself to be a loving sister and patient nurse. Her mother and father said, "Clara seems to be a born nurse," and she answered, "A nurse is what I am going to be."

When she grew up she studied nursing and became very skillful. She worked hard during wars in America and in the countries of Europe.

Once, when visiting in Switzerland, she learned about the Red Cross. As soon as she came back to America she went to see the President of the United States. She told him what she had learned in Switzerland.

Soon afterward, Clara helped to form the American Red Cross. We are all proud of Clara Barton and glad that the American Red Cross has been of great service to the country.

PART III

CONTENTS

THE UNKNOWN ARTIST

–A TRUE STORY–

Characters:

MURILLO   ....A famous artist

SEBASTIAN   ....Murillo's slave

FERDINAND, PHILIP, BELTRAN and
ANTHONY   ....Murillo's pupils

Place: The Studio of Murillo

SCENE I

Murillo's pupils are standing before an easel,
admiring a beautiful picture.

FERDINAND: Yes, this is my easel and this is my canvas, but as you can plainly see, the work is not mine. Last night when I left the studio the canvas was bare. Now look at the beautiful picture that covers it!

PHILIP: Who could have done it?

ANTHONY: I cannot tell, but one thing is sure. Whoever painted that picture is a *real artist.*

BELTRAN: Well, that proves that none of us did it.

Murillo enters and walks toward the easel.
The pupils do not hear him.

PHILIP: I believe this is the work of the master. See the color and------

MURILLO:	(Interrupting) What is this? Who brought that canvas in here?
BELTRAN:	It is Ferdinand's canvas, my master.
MURILLO:	Ferdinand! Did you paint that picture, Ferdinand?
FERDINAND:	No, master. You know I could never do such work.
MURILLO:	Beltran, is the work yours?
BELTRAN:	I! If I could paint like that I should be master and not a pupil.
MURILLO:	Philip, sometimes the beauty of your work surprises me. Is the picture yours?
PHILIP:	No, master. The one who painted that picture is a greater artist than I shall ever be.

Murillo lays his hand on Philip's shoulder.

MURILLO:	You may be right, my lad. Still, you will become a true artist. Anthony, do you know who painted this picture?

ANTHONY:	No, my master, unless it is the work of your own hand.
MURILLO:	No, my lad, it is not my work. Someone has painted it while we were away from the studio. I will find out who was here last night. Sebastian! Sebastian!

Sebastian enters.

SEBASTIAN:	Yes, my master.
MURILLO:	Who was in this studio last night?
SEBASTIAN:	I, master.
MURILLO:	Who else?
SEBASTIAN:	No one, master.
MURILLO:	Nonsense! Someone must have come in last night while you slept. Tonight watch carefully and tell me in the morning who comes into this room. If you cannot tell me what I want to know in the morning you shall be punished with thirty lashes.

SCENE II

The next morning Sebastian is standing before the picture just as the light creeps into the room. He holds a palette and brushes.

SEBASTIAN: Three hours till my master comes! I must blot out this picture before he sees it or he will have me whipped.

Sebastian holds the brush over the canvas.

SEBASTIAN: No! No! I cannot do it. I cannot blot it out. I will finish the picture and take the punishment.

He paints quickly.

SEBASTIAN: When I am painting I am happy. I forget that I am a slave. I feel as free as the birds.

The door opens softly and Murillo and his pupils creep up softly behind Sebastian.

PUPILS:	Wonderful! Beautiful!
BELTRAN:	Sebastian, the unknown artist!

Sebastian drops the palette and brushes
and stands trembling before them.

MURILLO:	Do not be afraid, Sebastian. Tell me, who is your master?
SEBASTIAN:	You, sir.
MURILLO:	I mean your painting master or teacher?
SEBASTIAN:	You, sir.
MURILLO:	Sebastian, tell me the truth. You know I have never given you one lesson.
SEBASTIAN:	No, master, but you gave lessons to your pupils and I couldn't help hearing you. And I wanted-- Oh! You don't know how I wanted to paint! And when I was alone I could not help trying. I had to paint! I just had to! I know it was wrong and you can punish me as much as--

Murillo throws his arm around Sebastian's shoulder and
turns to his pupils.

MURILLO:	Does this boy deserve punishment?
PUPILS:	No! No! No! No!
BELTRAN:	He deserves a reward!
MURILLO:	What shall the reward be? I shall let you decide.
ANTHONY:	A new suit of clothes. See how worn those are.
FERDINAND:	A purse of gold.
PHILIP:	Lessons with you, master.
BELTRAN:	Freedom, master! Give the boy his freedom!
SEBASTIAN:	Oh, master! Give freedom to my father!
MURILLO:	Do you not want your own freedom, my boy?
SEBASTIAN:	My father's first, sir.
MURILLO:	Your father shall be free, and you, too, my lad. You are free now, free to go wherever you wish.
SEBASTIAN:	No, master, only free to serve you for all my life.
MURILLO:	Then stay and study and paint with my pupils. We are proud of you, and

someday the whole world will be proud of the marvelous paintings of Sebastian Gomez.

- THE END -

JOSIAH BREEZE'S THANKSGIVING

– A NEW ENGLAND LEGEND –

Characters:

EZEKIEL BREEZE..........A fisherman

JOSIAH BREEZE............ Ezekiel's son

GRANDFATHER & GRANDMOTHER BREEZE

NEIGHBORS

CAPTAIN CLARK..........of the British ship *Ajax*

Place and Time:

Cape Cod, during the American Revolution

SCENE I

Ezekiel and Josiah are seated before the fireplace in their cottage. Ezekiel is mending a large net and Josiah is whittling a boat.

EZEKIEL: A wild night! I pity any ship that's off the coast tonight. This is the worst storm we've had since the night the *Nancy Bell* was driven on the reef and all her men drowned.

JOSIAH: I only hope the storm will pass before morning, so that we can go to Provincetown. It would not seem like Thanksgiving Day to me if we did not spend it at Grandfather's house.

EZEKIEL: This gale is too fierce to last long. It will wear itself out by morning----

A neighbor bursts into the room.

NEIGHBOR: A British ship! And it's a three decker! She's drifting toward land!

The neighbor rushes from the room.
Ezekiel and Josiah spring to the window
and peer eagerly into the night.

EZEKIEL: There she is! I see her! See the three red lights beyond the bluff!

JOSIAH: Oh, why don't they put out to sea! They will be lost!

EZEKIEL: They don't know our channels.

JOSIAH: I do. I'm going out to the ship.

EZEKIEL: No, Josiah!

JOSIAH: But she is in danger, Father. By morning she will be dashed to bits and strewn along the shore.

EZEKIEL: My boy, she is the enemy! Don't you remember how the men from the *Ajax* came ashore and burned the homes of our farmers and fishermen? Don't you remember how that big red-faced sailor, who was stealing Granny Brown's chickens, struck you with his cutlass when you tried to drive him away?

JOSIAH: But the men! Oh, Father, I cannot stand still and see all those men go down. Tomorrow in England there will be five hundred mothers weeping for their sons. And tomorrow is Thanksgiving! I just have to go, Father, and I will!

Josiah rushes from the room.

EZEKIEL: You're right, son; you're right. Wait, my boy, I'll go with you.

He runs to the door.

EZEKIEL: Josiah! Josiah!

Hearing no answer, he too rushes into the night.

SCENE II

It is Thanksgiving Day at Grandfather Breeze's home in Provincetown. Grandmother Breeze is finishing setting the table. Grandfather Breeze walks back and forth from the fireplace to the windows.

GRANDMOTHER: Do sit down, Father. They won't come any the sooner for your fussing.

GRANDFATHER: I know, I know. But aren't they late?

GRANDMOTHER: No. The turkeys won't be ready for a good hour yet. Do sit down, Father.

Grandfather is just about to seat himself in his easy chair by the fire, when the door opens and Ezekiel staggers in. He speaks no word but stumbles to the fireplace and stands leaning against the mantel with his head buried in his arm. Grandmother hurries to him and throws an arm around his shoulders. Grandfather seizes one of his hands.

GRANDMOTHER: What is the matter, son?

GRANDFATHER: My boy! What is wrong?

EZEKIEL: Oh, Josiah! My Josiah has drowned! He went out last night to help the men on a British ship. I would have gone with him, but he was off before I could overtake him. His boat, bottom up, was washed ashore. My brave boy!

The door is thrown open and several excited neighbors enter.

1st NEIGHBOR: A British ship, covered with ice, is sailing into the harbor.

2nd NEIGHBOR: See the hundreds of bluejackets on her decks.

3rd NEIGHBOR: Her pilot knows his business. How steadily he keeps her in the channel!

4th NEIGHBOR: Why, it's the *Ajax!* See they are sending a boat ashore. Get ready, men! We'll pay them back for robbing our people and burning our homes!

5th NEIGHBOR:	Aye, we'll get even at last.

The neighbors leave. Ezekiel and his parents return to the fireplace. Not a word is spoken. Again the door opens and in rushes Josiah, followed by Captain Clark of the "Ajax" and all the neighbors. Josiah grasps his father's hands.

JOSIAH:	Father!
EZEKIEL:	My boy!
CAPTAIN CLARK:	Aye, and he is a boy to be proud of. To save an enemy's ship, that boy put out in a sea few men could face.
JOSIAH:	Yes, father, and the enemy is brave, too. Captain Clark could have been miles away by now, but he knew you would be worrying about me, so he risked capture to bring me back. Oh, Father, isn't today a true Thanksgiving Day?
GRANDFATHER:	It is! Let us forget the war for today and just be thankful. Stay with us,

Captain Clark, and share our Thanksgiving dinner. Mother's turkeys must be ready now.

With happy faces and many handshakes,
all seat themselves at the table,
as the curtain falls.

- THE END -

PART IV

CONTENTS

PICNIC PIES

The Brown and Barnes families were going to have a picnic at Fern Hollow. Mrs. Brown had been busy all day baking cakes and cookies, frying chicken and preparing other good things.

She was going to have some pies, for all the children were very fond of them, but she wanted to make them the last thing, because she knew they would be best if they were eaten fresh. So it was late in the afternoon before she was ready to make them.

"Well, children," she said at last, "I think I'll soon begin to make the pies, then everything will be ready so that we can start early in the morning. What kind shall we have?"

"Currant," said Percy.

"Raspberry," said Bess.

"Cherry," said Rose.

"Well, children," laughed Mother, "we can't have them all. Which shall it be?"

After they had talked for some time and the matter was not decided, Mother said, "I'll tell you what I'll do. You may each gather the fruit you want and I'll make the pies of that which is ready first. Bess must pick the raspberries, Percy gather the currants and pick them off the stems, and Rose must pick and stone the cherries. Now we'll see who gets his fruit ready first."

Rose picked up a tin pail from the table, bounded through the gate, down the garden path, and was out of sight in a minute.

"Well," said Percy, "we'll have currant pies, you can be sure, for Rose has to go way to the other side of the orchard to pick the cherries, and then just think how long it will take to stone them."

"Bess doesn't have to go so far, but raspberries are little and they are so soft it will take a long time to pick enough for half of a dozen pies, and then the bushes are so high and thorny it will be slow work."

"All I'll have to do will be to sit under a big currant bush and scrape off the currants, for they are just thick. Then it won't take long to strip them off the stems. Hurrah for currant pies!"

"I know a place where the raspberries are thick, too," said Bess, "and when they're picked, they're all ready to use. I won't have to do anything more to them, so I think you'd better say, 'Hurrah for raspberry pies!'"

"Well, we'll see," said Percy. "How many currants shall I pick, Mother? Will this pail full be enough?" he added, picking up a pail from the table.

"Come on, Percy!" called Bess as she ran down the garden.

"I think I can guess what kind of pies we'll have," said Mother, with a funny little smile.

"Which kind?" said Percy.

"Never mind, Percy," said Mother, "just run along now and pick your currants."

Percy ran on after Bess and overtook her half way across the garden.

"What was that?" said Percy, as he stopped beside Bess. "I thought I heard Bert's whistle. That's what it was, and there's Bert now," he added, dropping his pail and taking a short cut through the corn patch to the other side of the garden to where Bert stood looking over the high board fence.

"See, Percy," said Bert, "here's the book Joe promised to lend us, and I thought we could sit out here under the big oak and look it over -- come on."

"Oh, Bert, I can't!" said Percy, "I'm going to pick currants for Mother, but put it up here on the fence and we'll have a look at it for just a minute." So Bert put the book on top of the fence and they began to look at the pictures.

"Percy," called Bess, running down to the berry patch at the other end of the garden, "I'm not going to wait for you another minute."

Percy, suddenly remembering the pies, jumped down from the fence saying, "We'll have to look at it some other time. I must go." Running back across the garden and picking up his pail, Percy was soon seated under a large currant bush picking away busily.

The currant and raspberry bushes were so near each other that Bess and Percy could talk as they worked.

Presently Percy called out: "How are you getting along, Bess?"

"Pretty well," answered Bess, "my bucket is half full."

They worked away quietly for a while till Bess said excitedly, "Oh, Percy! What do you think I've found? The dearest little bird's nest. I know it's an old one, so it will be all right for me to have it. Do come and help me get it."

Percy was over at the raspberry patch in a minute, and with Bess's help had soon pulled the nest from the thorny bushes.

"Take care," said Bess, as Percy stepped back from the bushes to hand her the nest, but she was too late. One of Percy's feet went right into the pail of raspberries, tipping it over so that about half the berries went rolling away under the bushes.

"Of course," said Bess, half crying, "you'll come out ahead now, for half my berries are gone and I'll have to do my work over."

"No," said Percy, "that was my fault and I'll help you till you have as many as you had before."

So they both worked till the pail was as full as before the berries were spilled. Then Percy went back to his currants.

When his bucket was full, he began to pick the currants off the stems and had just finished when he heard Bess go past him up the garden path as hard as she could run.

"Oh, you'll not beat!" said Percy, as he started after her. Just before she reached the house, he passed her and bounded into the kitchen about three steps ahead of her.

"Here are your currants, Mother," he cried. "Didn't I tell you we'd have currant pies?"

"Oh," said Mother, with that same odd little smile, "the pies are already made!"

"Why, Mother!" said Percy, reproachfully, "you said you'd make them of the fruit that was ready first."

"So I did," answered Mother, as she turned and took two pies from the oven, "and that is exactly what I have done -- we are to have cherry pies, Percy."

"*Oh!*" said Percy and Bess at the same time.

As they turned from the kitchen and went out into the yard, each one doing some quiet thinking, they saw Rose over under the trees swinging as high as the swing would go.

"Oh, Rose!" called Percy, "how did you happen to beat us?"

"I don't know," said Rose, "I just went right to work and never stopped till I had enough."

"Well, I don't understand it," said Percy, "you had so much farther to go and then all the cherries to stone. I don't understand it."

"I think I do," said Mother. "And so do I," said Bess, "and I'm sure Percy will too, if he thinks a little."

PRESERVED
ROSES

Jennie and Grandma and Uncle Ben lived together on the farm a little distance from the village. There were many wonderful, interesting and delightful things at the farm, and Jennie had a very happy time; but that which she enjoyed most was Grandma's rose garden, which Uncle Ben's untiring care made the most beautiful spot for miles around.

In the spring Jennie spent hours in the garden admiring the many kinds of roses and watching the buds unfold. She was especially fond of a certain pink rose the buds of which opened slowly and were perfect in shape and color.

"Grandma," she said one day, "the strawberries and the peaches and the cherries are beautiful, and I am always glad when I see you preserving them, for in that way we are able to keep them and enjoy their beauty a little longer. I wish there were some way of preserving these beautiful roses."

Grandma smiled. "Well, little girl," she said, "perhaps you can find a way."

Jennie did a good deal of thinking and several days later came to Grandma with eyes shining.

"Oh, Grandma," she said, "I've thought of a way to preserve the roses!"

Grandma laughed this time. "Well, dearie," she asked, "how are you going to do it?"

"I don't want to tell just yet," said Jennie, "but if you will let me have that pink rose bush down in the corner of the garden to do with just as I like, I'll tell you how after a while."

"Certainly," said Grandma, "you may have the bush."

"Even if I ask Uncle Ben to dig it up for me?" said Jennie.

"Yes," answered Grandma, "you may have it for your very own."

"I'm so glad," said Jennie, "and I'll ask Uncle Ben to let me know just as soon as the time for transplanting roses comes."

Some time after, when Uncle Ben came in to lunch one day, he said to Grandma, "I've just been transplanting Jennie's rose, and you'll never guess where she's put it. Away down by the wheat field along that dusty stretch of road, where there is not a tree nor a bit of shade of any kind."

"Why did she put it there?" asked Grandma.

"I don't know," answered Uncle Ben; "she said she wasn't ready to tell me yet."

With Uncle Ben's kindly help the rose bush grew

and flourished as well by the road side as it had in its old home in the garden, and Jennie watched and cared for it every day. She carried it little buckets of water, picked off the dry leaves and loosened the dirt about its roots just as Uncle Ben showed her.

Jennie was delighted when the little leaves began to come in the spring. Soon the bush was covered with opening buds and flowers. It was very beautiful and Jennie's loving care kept it as fresh and clean and sweet as it had been in the garden.

One hot, dusty day Jennie climbed down from the old apple tree by the gate, where she had been sitting all morning, and ran to Grandma, who was reading on the porch. "Grandma, Grandma," she cried, "some of my roses are preserved!"

"Are they?" said Grandma. "How?"

"Well," said Jennie, "a few minutes ago a man passed by the gate and went on down the road toward my rose bush. He was walking and carrying a heavy pack on his back. He didn't look very happy. He looked as if he were thinking of the long and hot and dusty road.

"I watched him and wondered if he would see my rose bush, and sure enough, he did, and walked straight up to it. He dropped his pack and stood looking at the roses and smelling them for a long time. Then he picked up his pack and went on.

"Do you know, Grandma, he stayed there so long that I believe he looked at every rose on the bush and I am sure for at least a part of the rest of his journey he will be seeing the roses and not the hot, dusty road, and if he keeps the roses in his thought, isn't that preserving them?"

"Yes, indeed," said Grandma; "but I hadn't thought of it that way."

"There was one thing that troubled me about it," said Jennie. "I hoped he would pick some of the roses, but I suppose he thought he had no right to them. I shall have to put up a sign by the bush."

In the afternoon Grandma found Jennie busy with her paints and brushes. "What are you doing?" she asked.

"Painting a sign to put up by my rose bush," answered Jennie. Then she held up a large piece of cardboard on which Grandma read:

> THESE ROSES ARE FOR YOU.
> PLEASE HELP YOURSELF, BUT BE CAREFUL
> NOT TO SPOIL THE BUSH.
> --JENNIE

Then Jennie ran down the road, fastened the sign to a stick, and set it beside the rose bush.

Every day she sat in the big apple tree by the gate reading, or watching the people who passed by. One day she saw a huge object coming down the road in the distance. As it came nearer she saw that it was a great load of hay which was so heavy that the horses could hardly draw it.

The driver, who was walking beside the horses, was very impatient with them because they seemed to find the load so heavy. When he came to the rose bush, Jennie saw him stop and give the horses a rest while he read the little sign. Then he picked several roses and pinned them on his coat.

As he came on past the gate and the apple tree, Jennie noticed that he seemed to be thinking, and did not call to the horses so loudly and impatiently as before.

"There," thought she, "some more of my roses are preserved --- he's thinking of the roses and not how slow the horses are and how hot and dusty the road is."

Another day as she sat in her tree watchtower she saw a carriage dash by drawn by a pair of beautiful black horses. The face of the man who was in the carriage showed that his thoughts were not pleasant.

Just then, he caught sight of Jennie's sign and drew up the horses that he might read it. Jennie watched him get out of his carriage, pick a bunch of the roses, and then, after standing there a long time, get in again and drive slowly on.

In the evening when Jennie went to water her rose bush, she found a little note pinned to her sign. As soon as she opened it, she knew it had been left by the man in the carriage.

The note read:

To Jennie:

I am helping myself to your roses and am writing this little note to tell you that I shall never forget them, for they have helped me to put aside some ugly thoughts that were making me very unhappy.

Gratefully,

Your Friend

"There, there, Grandma!" cried Jennie joyfully, as she ran to Grandma with the note, "haven't I found the way to preserve roses?"

"I think you have dear," answered Grandma as she fondly patted Jennie's radiant face.

BILLIE'S LION

As Billie's father was very fond of telling stories, and Billie was very fond of hearing stories, they had many good times together.

One morning when Billie and his little brother Don were having some trouble getting along, their father said, "Billie, would you like me to tell you a story?"

"Of course I would," said Billie eagerly.

"Well," said his father, as Billie settled himself in the big chair, "once upon a time, as a man was traveling through a wild country covered with forests, he found a baby lion by the roadside. It looked like a big kitten and Mr. Man got out and took it into his buggy with him. He carried it home with him and turned it loose in the house with his children. The children played with it several days and found it as gentle as a kitten.

"One morning a woodman who lived not far away called to see Mr. Man. 'Why,' he said, 'where did you get that baby lion? Why do you keep him here?'

" 'I found it in the woods and it is perfectly harmless,' said Mr. Man.

" 'I know it seems harmless now,' said the woodman, who knew a great deal about animals, 'but it will grow. After a while it will begin to lose its baby ways and to show it is a lion.'

" 'Oh, I don't believe it will ever do any harm. I am sure I can always manage it,' said Mr. Man. 'I don't want to give it up.'

"So Mr. Man kept the lion, and the children continued to play with it. Several times the woodman said, 'I wish you'd take that lion back to the woods where he belongs. Someday you'll be sorry you kept him.'

"But Mr. Man only laughed and said, 'He'll never do me any harm – I'll always be able to manage him.'

"By and by the lion began to be cross occasionally. He growled and waved his tail like a big cat.

" 'Now,' said the woodman one day, 'won't you be sensible and send that lion away before he does harm to someone?'

"Mr. Man laughed again and said, 'I'm not afraid.' So the woodman said no more.

"After this he came over to see Mr. Man one day and heard a great noise long before he reached the house. He hurried on to see what was the trouble.

"When he entered the door he found a great commotion. Mr. Man had come in just in time to save one of his children from being hurt by the lion, and now the whole family was trying to drive him into the strong cage where he slept at night. With the help of the woodman, who had caught a great many lions, they soon had him safe in the cage.

" 'Oh', said Mr. Man to the woodman, 'I wish I had taken your advice – but it's not too late now. I'll send him away at once.' So the lion was sent away and Mr. Man never again wanted to have a lion in his home."

Billie was very quiet for a few minutes, and then he said, "Father, I know why you told me that story. I'm Mr. Man, the lion is the anger that I allow to come into my thoughts so often, and you are the woodman. I'm going to be wiser than Mr. Man. I'm going to send my lion away while he's little – not wait till he grows and does me or someone else harm. I thank you for the story."

THE
NEW BRIDGE

"Come, boys," said Mother, early one morning. "I have a basket full of eggs ready for you to carry to the store, and I want you to be back promptly at ten o'clock."

"All right," said Phil, "may Lucy go with us?"

"I think Lucy had better stay at home," said Mother, "for you boys can walk faster than she can."

"No," said Teddy, "Lucy can keep up with us any day. She's a fine walker. Please let her go, Mother."

"Very well," said Mother, "only be sure to be back by ten o'clock."

So off they went, Phil and Teddy carrying the basket between them, and Lucy and their dog Rover running along behind.

It was only a mile to the town, and they had soon reached it and delivered their eggs to Mr. Brooks, the grocer.

As they started for home, Lucy said, "Oh, Phil! Run back and ask Mr. Brooks what time it is. If it isn't too late I want to pick a big bunch of those bluebells along the road for Mother." So Phil ran back to the store, while Lucy and Teddy walked on.

In a few minutes, Phil overtook them. "It's all right," said he, "there is plenty of time to pick all the flowers you want." When they came to the bluebells, they all stopped and the boys helped Lucy till she had a big bunch.

Just as they were ready to start on, Harry Stone came driving along with his donkey and cart. "Hello, boys!" he said. "Have you seen the new bridge over the river? You know it's the most wonderful bridge in the country. It will soon be finished."

"Yes, I know," said Phil, "and I do so much want to see it."

"Well, jump in," said Harry, "and I'll take you over. I go by it on my way home."

"No," said Teddy, "we have to be back by ten o'clock, and we won't have time."

"Oh, come on!" said Harry, "of course, you'll have time. It's only a mile from here, and the donkey can go fast when he tries. I'll bring you back as far as this. Come on, Phil."

So Phil jumped into the cart, and off they went, leaving Lucy and Teddy to go home alone.

Somehow Phil didn't feel very comfortable in his mind as the donkey jogged slowly along the road.

"Harry," he said, "I'm afraid I shouldn't have come. I'm afraid we won't be back by ten o'clock."

"Oh, yes, we will!" said Harry, "and that bridge is a sight that everybody ought to see."

After a while they came to a little stream which the donkey had to wade across, as there was no bridge. The banks were very steep and the donkey didn't like to go down into the water, but Harry finally succeeded in getting him down, and they went splash, splash, over to the other side.

When they started up the opposite bank, the donkey decided that he wouldn't go any farther, and came to a stop so suddenly that both of the boys bounced out of the cart and into the water.

The water wasn't very deep, and so no harm was done, only they were wet through and through. Phil climbed into the cart, and by much coaxing and petting Harry led the donkey to the top of the bank.

By this time Phil felt that it was getting pretty late. "Harry," he said, "I mustn't try to go any farther. Let's go back."

"I can't get the donkey across the stream again," said Harry. "You'll just have to wade, Phil, and besides I'm as wet as can be. I'll have to go on home."

When Phil reached home it was just noon. Mother got some dry clothes for him, and then they sat down to lunch.

She didn't say anything. Phil wished she would. He ate his lunch, expecting every moment to see Lucy and Teddy. When lunch was finished and they had not appeared, he said, "Where are Ted and Lucy?"

"I sent them away," answered Mother, and then sent Phil into the garden to pull weeds.

Phil worked hard all the afternoon, wondering all the while where Mother had sent Lucy and Ted.

Late in the afternoon a big auto full of children came flying down the road and stopped in front of the gate. Out jumped Lucy and Ted and away went the auto. Lucy was carrying a great bunch of violets and Teddy had a big basket. They ran at once to the house, and Phil kept on pulling weeds.

In a few minutes Mother called him to supper.

When they were all at the table, she said, "Now, Teddy, tell us about your trip."

"Well," said Teddy, "first Mr. Oaks took us to River's Park. I tell you it's a fine place. We saw fifteen monkeys, and I don't know how many parrots. The parrots all talked at once. They said all kinds of funny things. 'Hello, boys, hello! Come again, please! Goodbye, friends, goodbye!' and many other things.

"Then we went to the big field, over by the woods, where the ground is just blue with violets. We picked all those," he said, pointing to the large bunch which Lucy had placed on the table.

"Next we had our lunch under some big trees, where a little spring of cool water was just bubbling out of the ground. My, but the cake and sandwiches were good! Mr. Oaks seems to know all the interesting places in the country.

"After lunch he took us over to the wild strawberry fields. You should have been there, Phil. I think there were wagon loads of berries, and everyone as sweet as sugar. You'll see when it's time for dessert, won't he,

Mother? And last, but not least, was our ride to see the new bridge on our way home. I tell you it's a grand sight.

"Well, Mother," he added, "we've had a fine day, and I think Mr. Oaks was very kind to do so much for the children of the neighborhood. It seems to me we've traveled a hundred miles today."

"Yes," said Mother, "I knew you'd have a good time. That was why I wanted you to be home by ten o'clock. Mr. Oaks said he couldn't wait for anybody who wasn't ready at that time."

When supper was over, Phil went out to bring in his wood. He didn't say anything, but he did a good deal of thinking.

DOBBIN'S TARDY MARK

The little schoolhouse in the Cloverdale District had a great stretch of green pastures and meadows on one side and the most delightful grove of oaks and meadows on the other.

Many of the children in the school came a long distance. Most of them walked, some came on wheels and a few came in carts. In pleasant weather the horses were fastened to the trees in the grove until the children were ready to go home.

During the whole year there had not been one tardy mark in the school and now that the morning of the last day had come, each child was there a long time before the opening of the school and anxious to see that every other child was on time.

When it was almost time for school to begin someone discovered that Robin and little Sue were missing. Robin and Sue were two little people who came in a cart drawn by good-natured Dobbin.

"Oh, dear!" said Fannie and Bess at the same time, "now we're going to have some tardy marks after all."

Then they ran to Miss Mead, all talking at once. "Oh, dear, Miss Mead! We're going to have two tardy marks after all – Robin and Sue are not in sight and it's almost time for the bell. What shall we do?"

"I don't understand it," said Miss Mead. "Robin

and Sue are always here in such good time. I think we ought to see if they're in any trouble.

"Ned, you'd better take your wheel and go to the corner and perhaps you can see them. The road is so straight from there that you can see almost to their house, and if they're anywhere on the road you will be sure to see Dobbin's white coat. Then you can hurry them up a little."

So Ned went off on his wheel and Miss Mead and the other children watched him until he turned the corner.

Just as the bell rang to call the children to line, one of the girls, who was watching from the top of the fence, called out, "Here they come! Here they come! They're just turning the corner."

Down the road came Dobbin as fast as he could come, with Ned on the wheel beside him. Robin and Sue jumped from the cart while Ned tied Dobbin to the hitching-post, and the three children marched in and took their seats with the others.

Then Miss Mead and all of the other children

wanted to hear the whole story.

"It was all Dobbin's fault," said Ned, "and you'll never guess what was the matter. As soon as I got to the corner, I could see Dobbin way down the road. I waited some time, but as he did not seem to get any nearer I knew he must be standing still, so I got on my wheel and rode to meet them.

"You know the trees along this side of the road are like a solid green wall. Since yesterday morning someone had put up a big sign freshly painted white, right against the dark green trees.

"When I got nearly up to Dobbin, I saw the sign and knew exactly what was the trouble. The sun was shining on the newly painted sign in such a way that it shone like the headlight of an engine. As soon as Dobbin had caught a glimpse of it, he had stopped and refused to go another step.

"Robin had coaxed and talked and at last climbed out of the cart and tried to pull Dobbin along. But Dobbin wouldn't move. He stood still, looking straight at the big light, thinking, no doubt, that it was a train and he would stand there until it moved on out of his way.

"Robin and Sue couldn't come and leave him, so they both sat in the cart. 'Come on, Dobbin,' I said, taking hold of his bridle and patting his head. 'There's nothing there to hurt you.' But Dobbin stood perfectly still, never taking his eyes off the sign.

"Then I saw I'd have to do something besides talk to Dobbin. I'd have to show him that there was nothing about that terrible looking thing to hurt him or anybody.

"So I walked straight up to the sign, leaned against it and rubbed my hands over it, all the while watching Dobbin to see what he was thinking.

"He watched me intently for a minute or two, then giving his head several good shakes, as if he said, 'Oh, all right! I'll go on now,' he took his eyes off the sign, and trotted off up the road."

"Yes," said Sue, "and if Ned hadn't come to help us I think he would have stayed there until sundown."

"Well," said Bess, "Robin and Sue didn't make any tardy marks, anyway, for they marched in with us and were in their places as soon as the others."

"No," answered Miss Mead, "but I think we'll have to put down a tardy mark for Dobbin, for he's still at the hitching-post and his place is in the grove."

The children all laughed and clapped their hands for joy that every child had been in his place at the right time for a whole year, while Ned went out to put Dobbin in his place.

IN BLACKBERRY TIME

Mark lived in a country where one could travel miles and miles and see nothing but great fields of corn. He had many good times, but those he enjoyed most were the long journeys to the woods ten miles away, where he went with Father and Mother three or four times every summer to gather wild blackberries.

There were so many pleasant things about these trips – first, there was the getting up very early in the still, clear morning, long before the sun was up, and then the long ride in the big wagon on a great bed of hay, or on his pony, Dapple Dee. They usually reached the blackberry fields before the dew was gone in the thick woods, and the air was sweet with the fragrance of mint and other wild things.

As soon as Father had found a suitable place for the horses and wagon, they all started out to find a good blackberry patch. They never had to hunt long for the woods were full of them, and they often found places where they could pick a big bucketful without taking one step.

Mark and his mother always ran a race to see who could pick the most berries. Sometimes Mark came out ahead, but Mother usually won, because she was taller and could reach higher than he.

When noon came they had their lunch — and Mother always had something especially nice for a blackberrying lunch — in some pleasant, grassy spot under the trees, and sometimes by a little brook of cool water. After lunch they went to work again and picked berries until time to start home.

They usually brought one or two tubs and took them home filled with berries, and Mother was always busy for several days after, canning blackberries, making blackberry jam, jelly and other good things for the winter.

The first time they went blackberrying during the summer that Baby Maud began to talk was one that Mark never forgot.

They got up that morning early, as usual, and Mark was so full of joy that they were really going that he didn't know what to do. He helped Mother get the breakfast, fed the chickens and cows and helped Father harness the horses.

Then, not seeing anything else he could do, stood by the gate thinking, and this thought came to him: "I know what I'll do. I'll play a trick on Father. I'll just fasten Dolly's bridle to the bucket and lower it into the well. Then when Father looks for it, it will be such fun to tell him it's so warm the bridle's gone for a drink. Of course, I'll get it for him in a minute."

Now, Mark knew that this was not the right kind of thought and he knew he should not listen to it, for he was very fond of playing jokes and had found that they nearly always ended in trouble for somebody.

However, he did listen, got Dolly's bridle and leaned with it in his hand over the well to pull up the bucket, when down went the bridle and Mark heard it splash in the water at the bottom.

"Oh, I wish I hadn't done it!" said Mark, but there was nothing to do but to run and tell Father about it.

Then he and Father worked with a rake on the end of a long rope, with sticks and hooks and all kinds of things to get the bridle, for of course, Dolly couldn't help draw the wagon without her bridle.

When at last they got the bridle the sun was up, and so they all missed that part of the ride which was most beautiful, the part that was to have been taken in the cool of the early morning.

"Mark," said Father, as they finished putting on

Dolly's bridle, "I wish you'd learn something from this. No good ever comes from jokes of this kind, and sometimes much harm and inconvenience. You've really spoiled the morning for the whole family."

Mark felt very much ashamed and told himself that this should be his last trick.

They got started, Father and Mother on the seat in front, Baby Maud on the bed of hay in the back, and Mark trotting along beside them on Dapple Dee.

Mark kept close to the wagon where he could talk to Baby Maud, for she was the dearest thing in the world to him, and no wonder, for she always woke in the morning with a happy, smiling little face, and was as joyous as a bird all day long.

When they reached the woods, Father found a good place for the horses, then he joined Mother and Mark, who were already busy picking berries.

Mark thought the berries had never been so big and so sweet before. He and Mother ran a race before lunch and Mark won. "I think it's because I'm getting taller, Mother, and can reach almost as far as you can," he said.

When all their baskets were full, Father said, "It's about time to start home. Mark, you'd better take Dapple Dee and go on ahead and feed the cows and chickens before dark. We'll come as soon as we get all the things together."

So Mark mounted Dapple Dee and started for home. Mother got the lunch things picked up, Father hitched the horses to the wagon and when everything was ready to start, Mother went to the shady place where she had left Baby Maud asleep on a blanket.

There was the blanket, but where was Baby Maud? She was not there. Mother called and called her. Then she looked among the trees and bushes all around, but could find no trace of her.

Then she went to Father and they both looked and called until it began to grow dark. They both tried not to be afraid, hoping every moment to hear the baby voice answer them.

At last Father said, "I don't see anything to do but to go home — maybe Mark will know something that will help us in finding her."

So they walked around bushes, under trees and over the little paths until they came to the horses and wagon. Then they soon were started for home.

It seemed a long, long ride, though Father made the horses go as fast as they could. Mother tried to be brave, but the tears kept coming.

When they drove up to the gate, Mark was standing in the door looking for them. He couldn't understand why they should be so late, as it had been dark several hours.

Mother jumped out of the wagon and ran to the house. "Oh, Mark!" she said, "do you know anything about Baby Maud?"

"Baby Maud!" said Mark. "What do you mean, Mother? Isn't she with you?"

"No," answered Mother, "when we were ready to start we couldn't find her."

Mark could see that Mother had been crying all the way home, and he began to be frightened, too.

"I don't know—" he began, and stopping suddenly,

he said, "Wait a minute, Mother," and dashed out of the door and down to the gate.

In a few minutes he came running back with Baby Maud in his arms. She had just wakened from her nap and was all smiles as usual.

"Oh, Mark, where was she?" asked Mother, as she took the little girl in her arms.

"Mother," answered Mark, "I'm ashamed to tell you. When I started from the woods I stopped to kiss Baby Maud — she looked so sweet as she lay asleep.

"Then I thought it would be a good joke to put her into the wagon so that when you looked on the blanket you wouldn't find her. I supposed, of course, that you'd find her when you came to the wagon. I never thought there would be any trouble about it.

"I pulled the straw over her, because it was getting cool, and I suppose that is why you did not see her. She slept all the way home, and was still asleep when I went to get her. Mother, I'm so sorry."

"Well," replied Mother. "Father and I have suffered a great deal in the last two or three hours, Mark."

"Mother, I know it," said Mark, "and I have learned my lesson. I promise you this will be my very last joke." And Mark kept his word.

A PONY FOR FRANK

Frank had always lived in the city until he went to live with Grandma and Grandpa on the farm at Willow Brook.

Everything was new and strange to him at the farm, and there were so many things to learn about and to do that Frank was delighted.

Grandpa had a great many cows and horses and sheep, and there were hundreds and hundreds of chickens, Frank was sure, besides turkeys and geese.

Frank was very busy all the time exploring the big farm and Grandma and Grandpa did all they could to make his new home a pleasant one.

One evening, while Frank was taking a ride up and down the road on Ned, one of the farm horses, Grandma said to Grandpa, "Don't you think we'd better buy a pony for Frank? He'd enjoy it very much."

"Yes, I think he would," replied Grandpa, "but don't you think we'd better let him buy one himself? Wouldn't it be a good plan to let him earn the money and buy his own pony?"

"Yes, it would," said Grandma. "I hadn't thought of that."

When Frank came in for his ride, Grandpa said, "Frank, how would you like a pony of your own?" Frank's eyes danced. "Oh, Grandpa, "that would be too good to be true!"

"Well," said Grandpa, "you may have one if you

will earn the money to buy him."

"But, how, Grandpa, can I earn so much money? It will take a great deal."

"Not so very much," said Grandpa, "and I think we can find a way. I want someone to help me about the chickens, and you can do that very nicely. The hens are making their nests all over the farm, and I want to train them so that they will make their nests in the chicken houses. We lose a great many eggs this way, because we never find the nests.

"You may have every egg you will find outside the chicken houses, and Grandma will pay you for them, or you may sell them at the store. If you break up all the nests you find and take away the eggs, the hens will go back to where they belong."

"Oh, Grandpa, that will be fine, and won't I have fun hunting the nests? When shall I begin?" said Frank.

"Begin today," answered Grandpa. "You know there is no time like the present."

For a number of days the hens kept Frank busy.

He would sit out in the barnyard and wait until he heard a hen cackle, then away he would go, and nearly every time he would find a nest. Some of the nests were full of eggs.

One day a big white hen flew down from the hayloft cackling as hard as she could. In a minute Frank had climbed the ladder and was looking for her nest. A number of other hens flew up and went cackling out through the window.

"Well, well," said Frank, "I wonder how many nests there are here!" By looking carefully he found six nests nearly full of eggs.

Frank was so excited he hardly knew what to do, so he climbed down the ladder and ran into the kitchen to tell Grandma the good news. Grandma gave him a basket, and he soon brought it back full of beautiful fresh eggs.

"It won't take long to buy a pony at this rate, will it, Grandma?" he said happily.

The next day he sat outside beside the big haystacks in the field in back of the barn. He had not been sitting there very long when a hen flew down from the very top of one of the stacks.

"How am I to get up there?" thought Frank. But when he went around to the other side, he found a ladder that went part way up, and there at the top of the ladder, from a nest in the side of the stack, a hen flew down.

By holding on to the hay he reached the top and found three other nests. Then he climbed the other stacks and found some nests on every one. Next he went out into the meadow and found many nests hidden in the tall grass and in the fence corners.

He soon became so used to looking for nests that he found them in all kinds of places. He discovered a number under the currant bushes at the end of the garden, and one in a big, old straw hat of Grandpa's that had become wedged between the branches of an apple tree. He found one in the trunk of a hollow tree, another in an empty barrel, and still another under the seat of a wagon that had been standing in the shed for several days.

Soon he had quite a good start toward buying the pony. One morning he came in with eyes shining, and said, "Oh, Grandpa, I've seen the pony I want! She belongs to Mr. Moss, and he says he'll sell her to me. She's a beautiful chestnut, and I shall call her 'Penny'."

"Yes, she's the one I was thinking of," said Grandpa. "That reminds me," he added just as Frank was turning to go back out the door, "do you remember the big brown hen that sat on that nest full of duck's eggs and hatched out ten fine ducks?

"Well, she seems to know they are not chickens and won't have anything to do with them. How would you like to take care of them and have them for your very own?"

"I'd like them very much, indeed," said Frank. And he took such good care of the baby ducks, and they were so tame, that they followed him all about the yard. In a few weeks, they had grown to be beautiful large ducks.

Grandpa seemed to be always on the lookout to find ways to help him in earning his pony, and his little store of money grew rapidly.

One day Frank thought he must have nearly enough to pay for his pony, so he got out his money and counted it. "Only a few dollars more," he said to Grandma, running outside.

Grandma was talking to Mr. Pond at the door, and Mr. Pond was saying, "Yes, Mrs. Pond likes your ducks so much that she thinks she must have a few of them. Can you sell her eight or ten?"

"No," said Grandma, "but Frank has some. Perhaps he will sell them to you."

"Yes, indeed," said Frank. So Mr. Pond went out to the barnyard with him, and soon had the ducks in his wagon. Frank went dancing back to the house with the rest of the money for the pony.

When he led Penny into her new stall in the barn the next day, and knew she was his very own, he was the happiest boy in the country all around.

DICK'S FOURTH

Dick's home was on a big farm a number of miles from town. In the spring and summer, when the men were plowing and planting the big fields and cutting and harvesting the hay and grain, everybody on the farm was very busy and sometimes no one went to town for many days, except when one of the men went in a hurry to do an errand. Then Dick usually went too. In this way he made many pleasant visits to the busy little village.

One time when the town was a wonderful place to Dick was the night of the Fourth of July. Then all the people in the town and from all the country round met on the Square in the middle of the town and watched the display of fireworks.

Dick's father always took him to see this display, and they stayed until the last firecracker had been shot off, and then drove home late in the evening.

The Fourth of July was one of the days to which Dick was always looking forward to with pleasure. One 'Fourth' he said to his father, "Father, since I have studied a little about our country and learned what the Fourth of July means, and why we celebrate the day, the firecrackers don't seem the same to me. All they used to say to me was 'boom, boom, boom,' and I liked them just for the noise.

"Now, since I know that the Fourth of July was

the day on which our country became free, the firecrackers talk in a different way. Now they say to me, 'free, free, free!' "

When the next Fourth of July drew near, Dick could hardly wait. At last, just the day before the 'Fourth,' Father said, "It's too bad, Dick, but I can't take you to the village tomorrow to see the fireworks display. Two of the men had to go away and that leaves so much extra work for all the rest of us, that nobody can spare a moment to go to town. The hay must be cared for, for if it should rain, it would be all spoiled."

For a while Dick had quite a struggle with himself. The sense of disappointment seemed hard to overcome. "Well," he said to himself after some time, "I'll just have to find some other good way of spending the 'Fourth'."

The next morning he helped Mother churn the butter and take care of the milk. Then he did all the other little things he thought she would like to have him do.

After lunch he said, "I think Gyp and I will just take a run up to the woods near the sawmill and see if we can find enough little smooth blocks to finish my train."

So away he went with Gyp beside him. "Well, Gyp," he said, as they bounded along over the delightful little path and under the great forest trees, "we're glad we live in a free country, anyway, even if we can't go to hear the firecrackers talk about it, aren't we?"

Presently they came to a clear place with tall trees around it. In the center of this space was a great flock of birds busily picking something from the ground.

"See, Gyp," said Dick, "somebody's been having a Fourth of July picnic, and all these birds are clearing the table by picking up the crumbs."

When the birds saw the boy and the dog, they spread their wings and sailed away. Dick watched them until they rose above the tops of the trees.

Then, looking down at the ground, he saw that three of their little comrades had remained behind. They were beating their wings against the ground, and trying to free their feet from something which seemed to be holding them down.

Gyp saw them as soon as Dick did and jumped and danced around so much that Dick had to make him lie down, that he might not frighten them anymore.

Then Dick went quietly up to where the frightened little birds were struggling and found that their feet had become tangled in a great bunch of wire netting.

Their struggles had only made the matter worse, and Dick felt that it would take a long time and very careful, gentle fingers to get the little feet out without hurting them. So he took one of the little birds in his hand and laid his hat over the other two to stop their struggling.

It was slow work, but at last the little songster was free, and as he spread his wings and sailed away from Dick's outstretched hand, he sent back a beautiful song of thanksgiving for his freedom.

Dick watched him for a moment, and then went to work to loosen the other little captives. This took a long time, but Dick felt that he was more than paid for his work by the delightful, joyous song which each sent back as he flew away to join his friends.

Then Dick and Gyp went to look for the blocks, so that it was late in the afternoon before they got home. When Father came in to supper, he said, "Well, Dick, has it been a pretty lonesome 'Fourth'?"

"Oh, no, indeed!" said Dick, "so many pleasant things have happened that I've never thought of being lonesome." Then he told Father about the little birds.

"And, Father," he said, "when I had taken off the wire and the little things found they could fly, they were so happy that they all sang their thanks to me as they flew off. And to me they seemed to be saying, 'free, free, free!'

"No, indeed! I have never had a more pleasant 'Fourth' than this one. I almost felt as if I were one of the men who started the Fourth of July, for I had helped a little in bringing about freedom. And I know that the little birds had much the same sense of gratitude toward me that I have toward the men who made this a free country."